NATURE WATCH

THE
LIVING
POND

Nigel Hester

FRANKLIN WATTS
London/New York/Sydney/Toronto

© Franklin Watts 1990

First published in Great Britain by
Franklin Watts
96 Leonard Street
London EC2A 4RH

ISBN 0 7496 0179 5

Editor: Su Swallow
Design: K and Co

Illustrations: ·
Angela Owen, Ron Haywood
Phototypeset by Lineage Ltd, Watford
Printed in Belgium

Photography:
Heather Angel 4l, 5l, 5r, 6tr, 7 (both), 8tr, 8bl, 9 (all), 11c, 13tl, 13b,
13c, 14c, 15cl, 15bl, 15br, 16 (all), 17t, 17 (centre inset), 18 (both),
19t, 21, 22 (both), 23 (all), 24t, 25tr, 26t, 28 (both); Ardea (P Avon)
27br, (I R Beames) 26b, (J Clegg) 10t, 11tr, 14cr, (B Gibbons) 12tr,
(J Mason) 11tl, 13tr, (P Morris) 15tr, 27t, 27bl; Chris Fairclough 17bl,
17br; Nigel Hester 6tl, 6bl, 8br; Hosking 6br, 20b; Susan Kinsey 4r;
Frank Lane Agency (R Tidman) 24br; NHPA (S Dalton) 25tl; Oxford
Scientific Films 15cr; Planet Earth (Nigel Downer) 8tl, 15tl,
(M Mattock) 5t, 19c (Peter Palmer) 12b, 14t, (M Sheridan) 12tl;
Survival Anglia (J Harris) 20tl, (M Tibbles) 20tr; ZEFA 24bl,
26 (top – inset), 26b.

Front cover:
Main picture and inset right – Heather Angel, inset left – ZEFA
A CIP catalogue for this book is
available from the British Library.

CONTENTS

WHAT KIND OF POND?

Do you have a pond in your garden? Is there a pond in your village or in the town park? What do you know about your pond? Have you noticed the plants that grow in the water and round the edge? Do any animals live in your pond? This book tells you about different kinds of ponds and about some of the plants and animals that you may find in them.

A pond is a small area of fresh water (fresh water is water that is not salty). Pond shapes vary, but the water is usually shallow, and plants can grow right across its surface. All kinds of creatures live on or in the water, or spend part of their life in the water. Ducks and other birds visit ponds to nest and feed, and some mammals live by the water.

A pond can be an attractive feature in a garden. It allows people to grow water plants, and attracts a variety of insects and birds.

Ponds in parks attract ducks and geese. They dabble and dive for plants and insects to eat. In spring, some species may nest among the plants at the edge.

◁ On hills, pools may form in natural hollows in boggy ground, or in holes where peat has been dug out for fuel.

▽ The village pond was once a drinking place for horses, and animals being driven to market. The pond was often sited at crossroads and used by villagers as a meeting place.

◁ Duck decoy ponds were made to attract wild duck for food.

Most ponds are man-made. Ponds in parks and gardens are made for people to enjoy. In the past, village and farmyard ponds were dug to provide drinking water for animals. Ponds were also built by streams to hold water for driving huge mill wheels. Large houses often had a stewpond in their grounds, in which fish were reared for food for the landowner and his family. These stewponds attracted wild ducks, which were trapped in nets to provide a meal.

Some of these ponds have since been filled in, but where they still exist they provide an important habitat for wildlife.

A pond sheltered from the wind but open to the sunlight can support a great variety of wildlife. You will find plants, fish, insects and other small creatures, and birds.

All the animals associated with ponds depend on the pond plants in one way or another. The plants provide food for plant-eating animals (called herbivores) such as water fleas. They in turn are eaten by other animals (called carnivores). Larger animals then eat the smaller carnivores. This link between plants and a series of animals is called a food web or chain. A thriving pond supports many food chains.

Wildlife in the water

△ Yellow iris
▽ Large red damselflies

△ Goldfish and duckweed
▽ A coot

A food chain

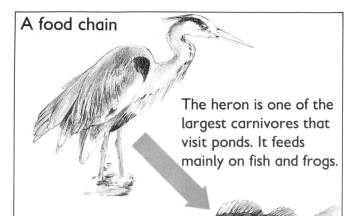

The heron is one of the largest carnivores that visit ponds. It feeds mainly on fish and frogs.

The perch eats small fish, beetles, worms and snails.

Some water beetles feed on plants, others on animals. The great diving beetle eats all kinds of animals, from small newts and fish to tadpoles.

Newts eat tadpoles, worms and tiny water fleas.

Water fleas and other tiny pond creatures feed on the microscopic plant plankton.

The plankton uses sunlight to make its food.

◁ If you go pond-dipping, put any creatures you find in plenty of water. They will die if they dry out. You could draw the animals before you return them to the pond.

▽ A magnifying glass is useful for looking at very small animals and plants.

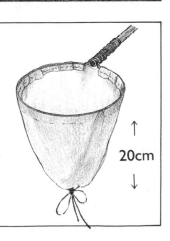

The best ponds to explore are shallow, with gently sloping sides and plenty of plants around the edge. Take care not to fall in, and handle plants and animals gently.

First, look for insects on the plants and on the water's surface. It is best to sit quietly and watch.

Next, scoop a pond net through the open water and tip your catch into jars or dishes of water. Put the insects and plants back when you have finished looking at them. Lastly, scoop some mud from the bottom to see what creatures you can find.

Making a net
Bend a wire coat hanger into a loop. Wind the ends round a cane and tie on with string. Sew a piece of old nylon stocking round the wire loop and tie the bottom tightly.

20cm

Pond plants grow in distinct zones. The marshy zone beside a pond is waterlogged. Plants that grow in this region usually have a spongy texture to carry oxygen. Other plants have their roots in the water at the edge of the pond. A bit further in to the pond, plants grow in the mud and have floating leaves. Plants in deeper water either float freely or are totally submerged under the surface.

Reeds are among the plants that grow at the edge of ponds. When these plants die, they fall into the pond. As the dead material builds up year after year, the water level is reduced. This area eventually becomes marshy and so marshland plants take root in it. In this way the pond gradually grows smaller.

Marshland plants

△ The trifid bur-marigold has fruits with barbed bristles. They hook on to the fur of passing animals, so the seeds are spread wide.

▷ The great reedmace produces fluffy seeds which are carried by the wind.

▷ Reeds *(far right)* have long, creeping stems in the mud, which prevents the wind uprooting them.

The shallow-water plants are not as rigid as land plants. Instead, they have soft, air-filled stems supported by the water, and leaves that sit on the surface of the pond.

Some plants are not attached to the pond bottom at all. They float freely, moving about in the wind. A dense bundle of roots absorbs minerals directly from the water.

△ The water soldier is a free-floating plant. In summer a chalky deposit forms in the young leaves. The extra weight makes the plant sink in autumn, so it can survive the winter.

◁ The yellow water lily is a common shallow-water plant. It is also called 'brandy bottle' because of the flask shape of its fruit capsules (inset).

Mapping your pond

A pond map will help you to study the plantlife. Fix strings on sticks on opposite sides of the pond. Mark the strings with knots of ribbon at 1 m intervals. Stretch two more pieces of string, also marked every 1 m, across the pond. By moving these strings along the fixed strings, you can study blocks of water 1 m square. Copy the shape of your pond on to squared paper, using one square for each 1 m block. Fill in the areas of different plants on your plan.

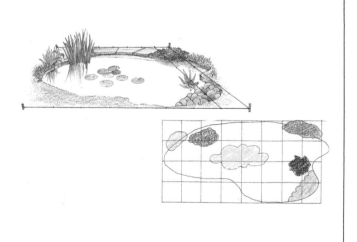

The deeper water of a pond supports plants that live under the surface. They all look very different from land plants. The water supports the weight of the plant, so there is no need for strong stems. Instead they have fine stems, which are easily broken. Their roots are small and either float freely or anchor the plant in the mud.

The leaves of submerged plants are also very fine. The leaves absorb carbon dioxide gas from the water, which the plants use to make their food. As the food is made, oxygen is released by the plant. On sunny days, look out for tiny bubbles of oxygen among the leaves of submerged plants. Plants need sunlight to make their food, too, so you will not see many bubbles on dull days.

The smallest plants in ponds are algae, which are related to seaweed. In warm, sunny weather, some algae rise to the surface of the pond to form a yellowy-green scum, called an algal mat. Like other plants, algae carry out photosynthesis in the sunlight to make food. They are an important part of the food web in a pond because many small creatures feed on them. Larger algae sink to the bottom when they die, where other creatures feed on them.

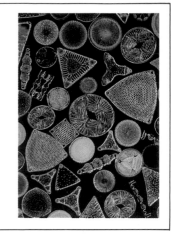

Did you know...?
Some algae, such as these diatoms, are so small they can only be seen under the microscope. The remains of dead diatoms, known as fuller's earth, are used in toothpaste, polishes and paints.

Plants for each zone

In the middle of the pond many plants grow under the water, although some flower spikes rise above the surface. Other plants in this zone float on the surface, with their roots trailing.

Plants nearer the edge of the pond have leaves which either float or stand out of the water. Some plants of the shallows have large leaves above the surface and fine leaves under water. Plants nearest the bank have long underground stems, called rhizomes, to hold them upright.

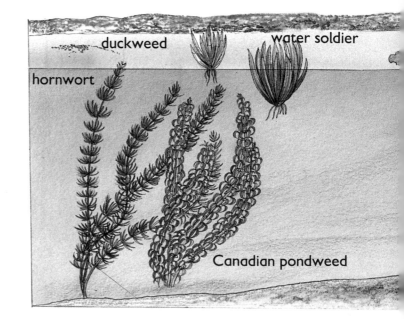

duckweed

water soldier

hornwort

Canadian pondweed

reeds

Some floaters

Hornwort *(right)* produces small flowers below the surface when the water is warm. Canadian pondweed *(far right)* spreads quickly. It can choke other plants, but provides oxygen for animals in the pond. The leaves of water milfoil *(bottom)* are very fine and grouped in whorls. The name milfoil means 'a thousand leaves'. Spikes of tiny flowers appear above the surface in summer.

great reedmace

trifid bur-marigold

marsh marigold

water lily

water plantain

water crowfoot

broadleaved pondweed

Many insects have adapted to life in or on pond water. The surface of the pond is a collecting place for pollen, leaves and dead insects. This debris forms a rich supply of food for tiny springtails, which in turn are attacked by pond skaters. Pond skaters use their pointed mouthparts to suck the juices out of their prey. Whirligig beetles spin round and round on the surface in search of prey. Their eyes are in two parts, for looking along the surface and beneath the water for food.

The swamp spider is not an insect, of course, but it feeds on them. It lurks in the plants at the pond edge until it detects ripples made by insects on the pond. Then it scurries across the water to dine.

Look for the pond skater *(left)*, the whirligig beetle *(right)* and the swamp spider *(below)* on the surface of the pond.

△ The great diving beetle can fly great distances. It is also a good swimmer. The water scorpion (above right) is easy to miss because its flat body looks like a leaf. Its long breathing tube could be mistaken for a leaf stalk. The great silver water beetle (middle) is the largest beetle in Britain (up to 5 cm long). It feeds on algae and traps oxygen in a mat of tiny hairs on its underside. The water boatman (bottom) swims upside down, using its legs like oars.

Most insects that prey on other insects keep to the open water. Water beetles are particularly fierce. The great diving beetle is one of the most powerful carnivores, quite able to deal with frogs, newts, and even goldfish. It is not a good idea to put one in an aquarium or even in a garden pond!

The young forms of most water insects (called larvae) live and feed on the pond bottom. A problem they all face is how to obtain oxygen. They cannot rise to the surface without risking capture. So some have feathery gills to extract the oxygen from the water, and others are able to trap oxygen bubbles in tiny hairs on their bodies.

Insects go through a number of changes before they become adults. Sometimes part of this life cycle is in water and part is on land. The early (larval) stage of many flying insects begins in fresh water, particularly in ponds. The larvae of mosquitoes and caddis flies, for example, are common in ponds. They look quite different from the adult forms.

The young of some other flying insects, such as dragonflies, resemble the adult form in some way. The young are known as nymphs.

Some larvae and nymphs are herbivores, while others are carnivores.

Mosquito larvae hang upside down from the surface of the water. They take in oxygen from the air, and trap food particles with bristles round their mouths.

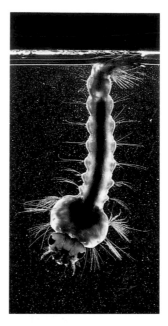

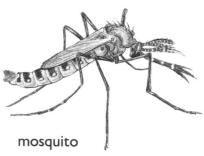

mosquito

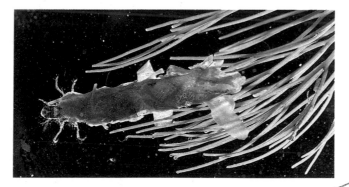

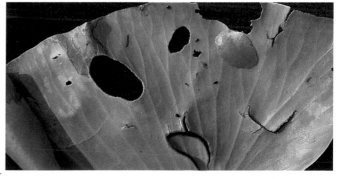

Caddis fly larvae live at the bottom of the water. They live in a protective case which they make out of sand, or bits of leaf, shell or twig. They stick the bits together with a silk from a gland near their mouth.

caddis fly

Some moth larvae live under water. The larva of the brown china-mark moth cuts pieces from floating leaves to form a case. Look for holes in leaves on the pond. Look on the underside of the leaf to find the larval case.

brown china-mark moth

The life of a dragonfly

Dragonflies start life in water. After mating *(picture 1)*, the female lays its eggs in the pond *(2)*. When the nymph hatches from the egg it feeds on water insects, tadpoles and fish *(3)*. As the nymph grows, it moults *(4)*, shedding its old skin up to 15 times.

When the nymph is ready to moult for the last time, it crawls up a plant stem and out of the water. The skin splits and the adult insect pulls itself out *(5)*. Look for empty nymph skins *(6)*.

southern hawker dragonfly

WORMS, LEECHES and SNAILS

If you hold a jar of pond water up to the light, you may see small worms wriggling about. Flatworms are simple animals with bodies covered in tiny hairs. They glide along the bottom of ponds by beating the hairs in the water. They feed on other small creatures, alive and dead.

Roundworms are very small but can be recognised by the way they thrash their bodies to and fro in an S shape. They feed on decaying material on the pond bottom.

Leeches are closely related to earthworms, with bodies divided into segments. Some feed on small animals, while others feed on the blood of larger animals. Some have three pairs of eyes to help them find their prey.

◁ Flatworms like this planarian have almost transparent bodies. Any colour comes from their last meal.

▽ Hair worms, a kind of roundworm, often form a tangled ball. Adult hair worms do not appear to feed at all.

The medicinal leech sucks blood from its prey. It was once used by doctors to draw blood from patients suffering from a fever.

In Britain, about 20 kinds of snail live in ponds. Some have gills for breathing, but most take air directly into their lungs from the water's surface.

Although snails are usually seen on pondweed, they rarely eat these plants. Instead, they feed on the layer of tiny algae that covers the pondweed. Not all snails are herbivores. The great pond snail, for example, eats small dead fish and other soft creatures.

△ The ramshorn snail is named after the shape of its shell. It dries up very easily, so it does not move from its pond. Other, smaller snails may be carried to other ponds on birds' feet. The great pond snail *(inset)* lays its eggs in jelly, on plants.

Watching snails

A freshwater aquarium is an ideal place to study snails. Watch them crawl over the sides, turning their heads from side to side. As they go, their rough tongues scrape off the algae which grow in a green film on the tank.

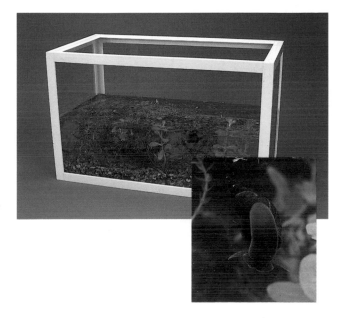

FROGS, TOADS AND NEWTS

Frogs, toads and newts are among the largest creatures found in ponds. They are all amphibians, animals that live mainly on dry land but also live in water, returning to water to breed.

The common frog has green, yellow or brown skin with dark blotches and lines. These markings act as a camouflage. The common toad is easily recognised by the warty lumps on its skin. Both frogs and toads shed their skin several times as they grow. They push the old skin off with their feet, and usually eat it.

 Frog facts
The African Goliath frog can jump up to 3 m.

 Some South American frogs can paralyse a monkey with the poisonous slime that coats their bodies.

 The eggs of a frog from Chile develop in the vocal sac of the male. When the tiny frogs are grown, they jump out of the father's mouth!

 The water-holding frog in the deserts of Australia absorbs enough water into its skin to last for up to two years until it rains again.

△ Toads lay their eggs about a month later than frogs, in chains up to 3m long. Some toadspawn may be eaten by frog tadpoles.

The natterjack toad *(inset)* is rare in Britain.

From egg to frog

In February or March frogs travel to ponds to breed. The males arrive first and croak to attract the females, which each lay more than 2000 eggs. Only a few eggs escape being eaten by herons, ducks, otters, foxes and other predators. When the tadpoles hatch, most of them are eaten by other pond animals. The tadpoles that survive develop into young frogs after 10-12 weeks.

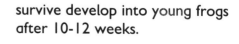

Newts are quite a different shape from frogs and toads. They are streamlined and have tails. They live in damp places. Newts die very quickly if their skin dries out.

The crested newt has a special defence against predators. Glands on its skin produce a strong-smelling chemical which irritates the skin of most attackers, although the chemical does not deter the grass snake from swallowing newts whole.

Newts spend more time in ponds than frogs or toads, staying in the water for up to four months to breed.

In spring, the male crested newt *(left)* develops a crest on its back and turns orange-red on its underside *(above left)*. It performs a special courtship dance to attract a female mate.

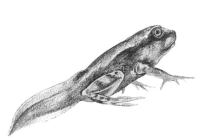

◁ The handsome mallard drake (male) is much more colourful than the female *(above)*.

▷ The reed warbler is a noisy singer. It chatters away for several seconds at a time.

▽ The moorhen swims jerkily, bobbing its head to and fro.

Ponds are important in the lives of many birds. They may visit the pond to drink, or to bathe. Some use the pond as a place to nest and rear their young. The reed warbler flies from Africa in the spring, and nests among reeds beside large ponds.

Many water birds have lost their homes as marshland has been drained for farming. Some water birds have adapted to these changes and now use man-made waterways. The mallard duck even nests by ponds in town parks.

UPLAND POOLS AND BOGS

High on the hills of Britain are large areas of moorland. Moist air and heavy rainfall keep the moorland very wet and the ground is nearly always waterlogged. Many plants are unable to grow in these conditions, but one plant that has adapted to this boggy habitat is bog moss, or sphagnum. Sphagnum has been growing on the wet hills for about 7000 years. Layers of dead sphagnum have built up in the ground to form peat, which is used as fuel for fires.

Boggy areas often have pools of open water, which support many strange plants. Some are carnivorous and obtain their food from animals.

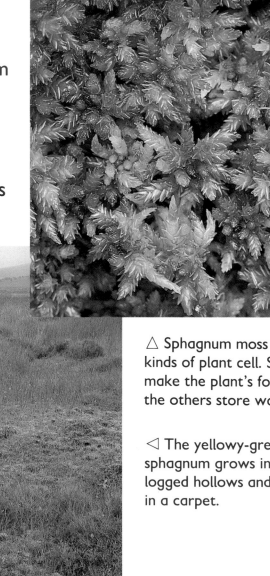

△ Sphagnum moss has two kinds of plant cell. Some cells make the plant's food, while the others store water.

◁ The yellowy-green sphagnum grows in water-logged hollows and spreads out in a carpet.

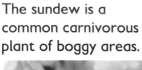

The sundew is a common carnivorous plant of boggy areas.

Insects are trapped by a sticky liquid produced by hairs on the leaves *(inset)*. Chemicals in the liquid digest the insect to provide food for the plant.

The bladderwort eats water fleas that get too close, attracted by the flea-shaped bladders!

water flea

▷ The large red damselfly visits upland pools to find insects, which it sometimes catches on the wing. It has large eyes to help it find food.

SMALL POOLS and DITCHES

Hollows in the ground fill with water when it rains. In cold weather in winter, the rainwater remains in these small pools. When the warm summer approaches, the water evaporates and the pool disappears.

Some animals have become so well adapted to life in temporary pools that they are not found anywhere else. The larvae of one mosquito, for example, live only in shady woodland pools.

The main predators in small pools are beetles. Some even breed in them, laying their eggs early in the year, before the water disappears.

△ Mosquito and caddis fly larvae live in this temporary woodland pool.

A bird bath
Birds often visit small pools to bathe. To make a bird bath, dig a shallow hole in the ground to hold a dustbin lid or large dish full of water.

▽ bullfinch

▽ The water vole lives in a burrow beside ponds and ditches. It is not a good swimmer but it dives well.

◁ Dragonflies patrol up and down dykes *(below)* in search of prey. Reed warblers nest in the reeds on the banks.

To drain wet areas of land, farmers dig ditches to remove the water. Today, there arc more than 80,000 miles of ditches in Britain. Ditches support a wide variety of wildlife.

Marshland that is used for grazing animals is often flooded in winter. Hedges will not grow in such wet ground, and wooden fences would rot. So farmers cut ditches round their land to mark field boundaries. Such ditches are called dykes, or 'wet fences'. Dykes are another important wildlife habitat.

Some plants grow so strongly in dykes and ditches that they can choke these valuable habitats.

▽ The great water dock, up to 2m tall, often chokes ditches.

The swallowtail butterfly, once common along dykes, is now very rare.

PONDS IN WINTER

Winter is the most difficult time for most pond wildlife, especially when the water freezes over. Some animals such as birds and insects can move away from the pond to find shelter. Animals in the water become less active so they need less food. Frogs and toads hibernate in the mud at the pond bottom, or elsewhere. Water insects, worms and snails move to the pond bottom, too, where decaying leaves protect them against the cold. Floating plants sink to the bottom to avoid the ice.

△ There is plenty of life beneath the ice of this frozen pond. Ducks stay on the pond if it does not ice over completely.

▽ The water shrew copes well in wintry pools. It feeds under water, but if food is scarce it hunts for earthworms on land.

Fish in summer and winter

Only a few varieties of fish are able to survive in ponds, because ponds have less oxygen than lakes and rivers. Carp are very well adapted to low levels of oxygen. In warm ponds with plenty of plants they can live for up to 50 years.

Like most pond fish, carp are bottom feeders, sifting through the silt and mud for food. In summer, carp eat algae. At other times they eat snails and insect larvae.

In winter, if the pond freezes over, fish rely on the oxygen produced by plants on the bottom. If snow covers the ice and blocks out the light, the plants produce carbon dioxide. Without oxygen, the fish die.

△ On a hot day, carp rise to the surface of the pond to bask in the warmth and to obtain more oxygen.

Carp *(bottom left)* and tench *(below)* feed in the mud at the bottom of the pond, even in winter.

PROTECTING PONDS

Ponds and other areas of fresh water are important not only as places for people to enjoy but also as homes for many plants and animals. Without ponds, ditches and streams, much of our wildlife would disappear. Since 1930, half of the freshwater habitats in Britain have been lost. Wetlands have been drained for farming. Ditches and ponds have been filled in. Others have been polluted.

Pollution is probably the most important threat to ponds and pondlife. Fertilisers from farms and chemicals from industry drain into the water and kill off the wildlife. It is important to save the areas of fresh water that are left.

Help to save a pond

Perhaps there is a pond or ditch in your area that needs care and attention. You may be able to clean it out with the help of your school or family. The best time to work on a pond is in the autumn, when the animals are not breeding.

The first task will be to clear away any rubbish that has been dumped in the pond. If the pond has silted up, then some of the mud should be dug out. Do this a bit at a time, to avoid removing all the wildlife hidden in the mud.

When fertilisers from farms enter a pond, some algae flourish with the extra food *(below left).* The algae reduce the oxygen level and animals die.

▽ Ponds that are used as a refuse dump certainly look unpleasant and soon become unsuitable habitats for plants and animals.

Make your own pond

The best way to help protect pondlife is to have your own pond. Perhaps you could make one in your garden or at school. Plan it carefully. Choose a site on level ground, away from trees so that leaves do not fall into it. It needs to be at least 2 m long, and 45 cm deep.

Potted and floating plants can be put into the pond as soon as it is ready. Wait for a few weeks before adding any animals.

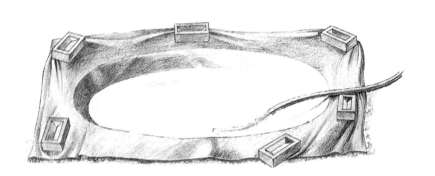

When you have dug out the pond shape, remove any sharp stones. A layer of sand on the bottom and sides will help to make a smooth surface which will not make holes in the lining.

It is best to buy a heavy-duty lining from a garden centre. Stretch the sheet across the hole and weight the edges down. As you pour water on to the sheet, it will sink down against the sides of the pond. Cover the edges with stones or turf.

To help you identify pond plants, notice especially the shape of the leaves and in which part of the pond they are growing.

Water plants provide food and shelter for many small animals. Look for insects on leaves and stems, as well as on the water itself.

To help you to identify an insect, make a note of its shape and size and the way it moves.

water crowfoot

reed

broadleaved pondweed

water lily

water soldier

trifid bur-marigold

reedmace

Canadian pondweed

southern hawker dragonfly

large red damselfly

pond skater

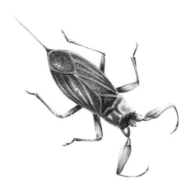

water scorpion

water boatman

great diving beetle

Spot the plants and insects

Now that you have read about ponds, test your knowlege and see if you can identify the plants and insects which have appeared at the top of some of the pages in this book. You will find the answers to the quiz on the next page.

whirligig beetle

mosquito

Answers to quiz:
Page 1 water soldier, p2 water lily, p3 water boatman, p5 trifid bur-marigold, p7 mosquito, p9 reedmace, p10 southern hawker dragonfly, p13 reed, p15 great diving beetle, p17 water crowfoot, p19 large red damselfly, p23 broadleaved pondweed, p25 pond skater, p27 Canadian pondweed, p29 whirligig beetle, p32 water scorpion.